Siftings

Psalms of the Heart
from
The Baker and the Bread

David W. Riordan

Siftings

Psalms of the Heart
from
The Baker and the Bread

ISBN: 979-8-9892190-2-5

Published by the Baker and the Bread
Chelsea, OK—thebakerandthebread.com

To M

And everyone who wishes
to know God
as I

Preface

I enjoy writing poetry, and I have a passion for sharing Christ and the hope of abundant living. When I get to combine them, wow!

Unfortunately, I'm not much of a poet. Occasionally, God gives me something good, and the words seem to flow unimpeded. The results are inside. My only hope in this is that He gives me more, but my hope for you is that you'll be encouraged to walk closer to and live a more robust life for, Jesus Christ, my Lord and Savior.

A Psalm is an "Expression of Worship," according to Bible.org. I can think of no better description. From 'To My Mom" to the tongue-in-cheek "Misery Loves Company," everything I've written here is simply to honor my Lord in worshipful expressions.

From gratefulness to sadness, and anger to happiness, with an occasional attempt at humor, I find the emotions of life worthy of placing into words. While we do not walk by our emotions, for we live by faith, when emotions follow the fact of faith, we discover not only the rightful place of emotion but the joy that is beyond elementary feelings. This joy consumes me even when depression knocks at my heart's door or anger threatens to overwhelm my mind. Faith overcomes it all and undergirds my existence with a peace that surpasses my understanding.

This joy that I speak of does not mean I do not face the ups and downs of life and the twists, turns, and emotional rollercoasters of relationships. I experience them all, but, like living in a well-stocked cabin built by a never-ending stream on a Caribbean Island, the replenishment of peace is only a few steps away. I may hunger, but I never starve; I might get thirsty, but a drink is ever near at hand; and I never face the emptiness and cold of the life I formerly lived.

Knowing Christ and trusting Him filled the void where I previously existed. Trust Him; He will never disappoint.

In Christ Alone,
David

To My Mom

My first love came when you took the lead,
And you opened a book and taught me to read.
Learning was paramount, you made me see,
You made it important every day on your knee.

Opening my eyes to greater things I should see
Because there were larger lessons than what revolved around me.
Before I'd seen what was beyond my home,
I could grasp what I might find when I began to roam.

You gave me a foundation on which I could build.
It was solid as the rock, the scripture instilled,
For reading opened a path to memorizing things,
Of wisdom, sanity, and songs I should sing.

Success in life is not easily found.
Most start their lives on sinking ground.
But you made sure, you opened my mind,
By setting me up to make an awesome find.

Life takes its turns beyond our control or whim.
By teaching me to learn, you taught me to swim.
No matter the storms or unsurmountable wave,
There's always an answer and the One Who will save.

So, things happen at the unstoppable speed of life.
There's heartbreak, pain, and with others there's strife.
I remember I broke my arm; you were there,
Holding back your own, so you could dry my tear.

Learning and the Bible were important things to know,
But in that moment of pain, you let your compassion glow.
I saw something else I would need lifelong:
The ability to give myself and make others strong.

But in the end when devastation wiped your mind,
There was but one thing left of you, and God gave me a sign.
Out of the thousand-yard stare that consumed your face,
You spoke your last words, and they were a message of grace.

It took me back to those times on your knee
When the quest for knowledge taught me to see.
Truth unbounded, love unfolded, in the lap of my mother
I learned the love of Another.

So, when I cried out, t'was not to an empty sky,
For I already knew Who, though just not the why.
Trusting the Trustworthy wasn't hard to do
When the lap I sat on belonged to you.

Alone

When a large number of people are hurting,
I may not be able to aid.
I am but one, as each of us are,
I must not be afraid.

Where to start or what to do,
The answer I struggle to find.
There's so much to do,
Good things to be done,
I must be gentle and kind.

I reach out to one, another rises up,
Overwhelmed I surely will be.
Better answers exist, I know that is true,
I must look outside of me.

I cannot do much alone by myself
To offer deliverance.
If I join with others, efforts are doubled;
We make a difference!

But in the end, it all comes to this:
To reach the world we must
Be led by the Spirit and work as one
And walk in complete trust .

It’s Who You Know

In front of the tent,
in the shade of a tree,
The old man and his wife,
no child could they see.

The prophets of Baal,
Defeated and scattered,
He ran and fled
From all that had mattered.

Prophecy spoken,
Sat under a leaf,
What fish didn’t do,
He wanted in grief.

He sat in his boat,
Torn nets he was mending,
He needed a change,
The catch would be ending.

It's certainly a fact,
And definitely true.
From Abraham to Peter,
And Jonah to you.

Where you are
Is where you are at;
Nothing can change
Or alter that

It's a place to start
From where you can go,
But it's not what you do,
It's who you know.

The good news I have
To tell it to you:
God met those men,
He'll meet you too.

There's nowhere to go
Where He cannot be.
In the darkest of night,
He's the light you can see.

So stop where you are
And cry out to Him.
You'll not make it alone.
You're out on a limb.

The good news I have
I give and I share.
Despite where you are,
He'll meet you there.

Just like those men
From times of old,
He comes right to you,
Brings you out of the cold.

So trust and rely.
His love is incessant.
Right where you are
Is where He'll be present.

He'll take your hand
And lead you out;
You need have no fear,
No worry nor doubt.

No matter your mess,
Your heartache or grief,
Please follow Him now,
He's your only relief!

When the time comes,
And you see what I say,
Don't forget to say thanks
For the rest of your days.

He's the God of power.
He'll always be there.
Just call out His name,
He's closer than air.

I hope it happens for you,
As it happened for them;
You must call out His name,
Forsake all, follow Him.

THE FIGHT

BATTLES COME,
OPPONENTS APPRAISED,
PREPARATIONS MADE;
WEAPONS RAISED.

THE NEED TO FIGHT
IS ALL TOO REAL,
DANGERS ABOUND
AS THE ENEMY STEALS

MOST DEFEND
AND CIRCLE THE WAGONS,
ANGST AND FEAR,
THE WORST IMAGINED.

I DON'T KNOW WHY,
THERE'S ANOTHER WAY,
OUR SIDE HAS A HERO—
NEVER FAILS TO SLAY.

DRAW SWORD IF YOU MUST;
IT'S SHARP INDEED,
DOUBLE-EDGED AND BRIGHT
A REQUIREMENT AND NEED.

IN THE END,
THOUGH NOT WON WITH EASE,
WE FIGHT BEST OUR BATTLES
UPON OUR KNEES.

WHEN WE'RE ENGAGED
BUT OUT OF THE WAY,
OUR CHAMPION STEPS IN AND
WINS THE DAY!

HE'S ALWAYS ON TIME,
NOT EARLY OR LATE,
PATIENCE, OUR TOOL,
VICTORY, OUR FATE!

Time

Time is the great equalizer,
and two things remain true.
60 seconds in every minute,
Is the same for me and you.

No more, no less
as we go through our day,
Each one of us must choose
How we go our own way.

We play, we work,
Sometimes help others too,
Decisions and compromise
Rule what we do.

Some do nothing
With the time they've got.
Wasting precious moments
The clock may allot.

Many are busier
Than a whole hive of bees,
Working very hard
Breaking back, scarring knees.

It matters what we do
As we all plan our days.
We should follow God's will
And do what He says.

The truth is stated:
we have the same time,
Seconds and minutes,
None less nor more prime.

There's one more thing
That remains to be said
For those who're alive
And not yet dead.

As the universe winds down,
And as predicted before,
One's about to stand up
And declare, "Time's no more!"

With time near its end
And eternity near,
We can decide
Driven by love or fear.

With only one breath,
We make the choice,
"Save me Lord Jesus,"
Lifting up our voice.

Exciting stuff
Lies in eternity,
But that's not now
Where our focus should be.

Abundance and Satisfaction
Our Lord promised us
In our day to day lives
If only we'll trust.

Walking with Him,
Always following His will,
We don't have to wait
To enjoy life's thrill.

Heaven will be awesome
Joy is all He will allow.
Salvation's for then
But it's also for now.

How we use time
Is truly up to us,
Lay aside every worry
And walk in complete trust!

Faith

Now faith is the substance
of what we can't see,
it's why we know what's right.
It's far more than feelings,
beliefs or thoughts.
It's the evidence behind hope and might!

When the world attempts to redefine faith
as less than what it is,
Our actions have spoken
much louder than words,
and our message they surely miss.

Our words unheard, our Gospel not heeded,
it really is a shame.
Most often the fault lies squarely on
the ones called by His name!

Repent, take action!
There's a desperate need,
our words have lost their power.
The ones who might hear, listen, and turn
are dying by the hour!

Overcome

I lose my focus.
My drive disappears.
Hope diminishes.
My eyes dry of tears.

What has happened?
I do not know.
Where do I turn?
What direction should I go?

I understand some.
I've been under attack.
From all directions pushed,
Trying to make me go back.

Forward I press on
Despite how I feel.
I'll go with what I know,
His Grace has been real.

What I know is concrete:
The evidence for my faith;
When I walk in His steps,
I have reasons to praise.

I will take a moment,
Remember all He's done,
The battles I've fought,
The victories He's won.

I have my struggles.
This I know is true.
With disappointments and trials
Still yet to go through.

If I want to grow
And become more like Him,
I must endure all,
Bear my cross made of them.

Though my load is heavy,
With burdens to bear;
It's nothing like His
I did not have to share.

So, press on I must
And count all things but loss.
Following my Lord (when compared)
has minimal cost.

"Snap out of the doldrums,"
Myself I remind.
Like sin, good actions
Begin in my mind.

Make the right choices
And begin anew,
Step into His purpose
With only His view.

Each day has its challenges,
I must not lose sight.
Beginning with Him
I'll overcome by His might!

Hands

Hands we have, what will we hold
To make us useful, for His purposes bold?
Created by design and certainly purpose,
What will we do when called into service?

Youthful hands held bloody sword,
Giant's head rolled like a gourd,
Roar erupts from those around,
Little David stands his ground.

Temple treasure in prophet's hand,
Hide it well in cave or sand,
Weeping loud, full of sorrow,
Looks ahead, promise of a new tomorrow.

Seasoned hands reel nets in,
Unaware of original sin,
soon to learn what's hard to swallow,
Peter yields, a call to follow.

Honey-stained palms, in skins he dresses,
Calls for repentance with uncut tresses,
Wrinkled skin in dirty water,
Head on a platter, king's dancing daughter.

Rings adorn with painted nails,
Water to draw, she fills her pails,
Soon to have, soon to hold,
Forever fountain, refreshing, cold.

Bloody hand the hammer holds
Soldier scorns, curses, scolds,
Knowing not his actions' bane,
Drawing back, he swings again.

Fingers bent over rusty spike,
Pain in hands and feet alike,
Tears of love fall down His face,
Sacrificed once, all sin erased.

Called to service, put hands to it,
Renewed minds led by the Spirit,
Hands tell a story, reinforcing the tongue,
What we do should honor the Son.

What do others make of your life,
Do your actions make peace or cause much strife,
Actions of love, hands doing good,
Make your words heard and understood.

Forgiveness

I don't think I've ever felt
As alone now that I've been dealt;
Another's sin has cost me dearly;
From one I loved truly and sincerely.

Sin has a cost, and it must be paid
By more than the one who masquerades.
It is a burden borne by more
Than only the one who's upped the score.

I labor alone, my thoughts are heavy.
Though tears should come, I've built a levy.
Holding back the pain and too much sorrow,
I'm hoping for a new tomorrow.

I cannot judge. I've done the same
Before the time He knew my name.
I hurt and broke everyone I knew.
I was no different before I was new.

I could have done more to shield myself;
Protect my heart, keep it on a shelf,
But if I did and held myself back,
Who would I hurt if my actions lack?

So push on I must, though I've been pained.
The anguish I feel, my love is stained.
It's hard to move when dashed by another
Upon the rocks, thrown by a brother.

Wrap up my heart and bandage tight,
Forgiveness is tough, but it is right.
When I hold it back from the one who's wrong,
Others suffer if I cannot be strong.

Unleash the love that God's shown me.
Follow this truth, and I'll be free.
And lead others out by what I do.
Repair their hearts and make them new.

Perhaps one day, the one who sinned
Will search me out and find me again.
Seeking to unlock the chains
That bind his heart from all that remains.

If he does, then he'll find me
Unshackled, unburdened and truly free.
I should not let the wrong of another
Hold me and stop me from helping others.

In the end, it is my choice
to hold onto hurt and lose my voice.
For today, I will let it go;
Forgive and forget and let tears flow.

I'll pray for him from this day forward.
I can release and move on toward
The things that God has in store for me.
Now that I've let go, I'll be able to see.

How Do I Write Sadness?

How do I write sadness, I do not know.
When life slings arrows from an evil bow.
It's bad enough when the hateful are mean,
But how do I handle the simple routine?

Everyday life is filled with sorrow,
Day after day, assured for tomorrow.
Awakening with only one last hope—
That today will be less and not more so.

Depression and anxiety are both in the mix.
Choose one or the other or stand betwixt.
What do I do when all runs amok;
Ruts in the road, and I seem to get stuck?

My head says there is abounding hope.
My heart chimes in just trying to cope.
How will I make it, how can I stand
If I lose my focus, never understand?

Wisdom is free, or so I've been told;
Open the door, come out of the cold.
It's hard to know when you're standing outside
How easy the answer when in Him you abide.

Alas, I know just what I should do
To find the way and make it through.
Knowledge is power, a very false claim.
The only true power is in His name.

Reliance, much harder to achieve for most.
I've been here before. It's not a boast.
A lesson hard won through stubbornness and pain.
His deliverance was sure, and nothing but gain.

Experience is a teacher, the builder of faith.
From what's gone before I can build my case.
Still knowing and doing are two different things.
It's why I'm in the dark with no song to sing.

I must let go of all that binds me.
Give it to God and set myself free.
Instead, perpetuating pain I remain in the dark,
Unable to move the shifter from park.

The switch on the wall is easy to flip,
Unable to move, further down I slip.
If only the light would come on by itself,
I'm sure I could improve and better myself.

Paralyzed by fear, I will not move.
I lay in silence, my heart unsoothed.
"Too much, too much," my brain screams aloud.
I cannot take more; no more is allowed.

Desperation moves my trembling lips to say.
It's the last thing to do, I finally pray.
No immediate relief from all my pain,
I slip on the hill; at the bottom's insane.

One thing's for sure, it'll happen at last:
The sun will rise as it has in each past.
A light will come on. He will make it so.
It's my glimmer of hope, a thing I know

It's all I can do from prone in my bed—
Swing my legs o'er and raise my head.
I'm still in the dark, just waiting to see;
A new day's light, a miracle for me.

Sometimes in the depths, it's all I can do;
Stand up in the dark and await the new.
But that is something, my feet on the land,
Having done all I can, I simply stand.

Sorrow's assured but so is good.
It's on His promises I've previously stood.
I must remember and move from my bed.
He certainly did more in my place, in my stead.

So, standing up, I will await Him
Regardless of my feelings and hope that is slim.
I'm at that point, not much to offer,
Depression's grip, my current scoffer

But stand I will, having been here before,
I will pull back the curtains and open my door.
I cannot make the light, the thing I need.
He can and will, I don't have to plead.

Waiting on the Lord is a hard thing to do,
His daily promises for me and you.
They are not empty, we can hold on tight;
He's the God of love, power, and might.

When darkness grips, and depression takes hold,
We have to remember or perhaps be told
That waiting is doing, it is an action we take.
When our focus is on Him, it's not a mistake!

Revival

A worldwide revival is coming,
the Church will arise again,
With hearts ablaze and souls on fire,
I wonder where it'll begin.
As the Church ignites and gifts abound,
The Body will unite as one.
Miracles will happen, and signs appear,
Eyes will look to the Son.
The world will take notice, it'll be hard to miss,
As Jesus steps from His Throne;
Those who've been seeking will surely find,
And the lost equally won.
This precedes a desperate time for all humanity,
As the evil man holds dominion and sway;
His goal our defeat, his vic'try.
We know this is coming, the clock has run out,
The signs and promises clear.
My wonder has an answer for where it will start,
For it's not further but near.
The first step to the world's redemption,
If I want to play a part;
I must turn my vision to only His will,
Revival begins with my heart.

Not an Option

What do I do when I just want to quit?
Things seem wrong, my fire's barely lit.
Attacked from all sides, wounded and harmed
I've sent up a flag, an all-points alarm.

How much more, I ask to the sky.
The sky has no answers, no reasons why.
I know what is real, what is definitely true.
I know where to go and just what to do.

But blocks are in place, I stumble and fall.
Pushed into the dirt, I've given it all.
Battered and bruised, I can't even walk.
My writing's been banned, it's hard to talk.

What will I do, I cry to my God.
No answer's apparent, I feel at odds.
If I must choose when no answer is clear,
I look to the things that I hold dear.

Perhaps my possessions hold a clue
to the things I feel are more important than you.
Release them I will for I have a choice;
I will give Grace and Mercy a resounding voice.

If Christ can give up Glory just for me
What should I choose to give willingly?
He set an example in all that He did
I must give up me and be like Him instead.

Anything that stands obstructing my way
over my thoughts and deeds hold sway;
those I must give up if I want His sight
To see my neighbor and do what's right.

Too often I'm tired and struggling,
holding tight to possessions is exhausting.
Not only do they wear me completely out here
I give up the treasure I hold most dear.

"Store up your treasure where rust doesn't corrupt,"
Is what our Lord said about how we conduct
our lives and actions toward others and such;
giving is storing; it's how lives we touch.

When I look beyond all that is me and mine,
My burdens are lifted, and I begin feeling fine.
But if I cannot see my neighbor next door
I hold what's blocking my eyes and more.

If I want joy and life to abound
I have to let go of what's lashing me down.
Untying my greed for all that I own
I give it away as seeds to be sown.

In planting life in those who I know
I set myself free, though the trials don't go.
I just no longer see them as what they were—
needs are apparent, they become a blur.

There's nothing wrong with having things
God gives us a lot in all that life brings,
But when they grow too important to see,
I value them more than Christ in me.

The secret to joy is the thing I've found.
Possessions won't follow us into the ground.
We don't stay buried for long anyway.
More awaits in Heaven than what we give today

Absent

How will I be remembered?
Will I be thought of well ?
For the deeds I've done and things I've said,
Will others my story tell?

I wonder what others will think
About the works I've done.
Writing words, feeding the lost,
And about the race I've run.

When my body is dressed and laid out
What will others say,
In mourning tears with praise on their tongues
On my dying day?

Will my funeral be packed, only standing allowed,
Or maybe there'll only one?
I don't know if songs will be sung
Before all is said and done.

The truth of the matter upon that day
Is that I will not be there.
Of what is said and all that is done,
I'll really not have a care.

At that moment and in that time
Before the Throne I'll stand,
The King will speak, say one of two things;
I will answer to His command.

So when I'm dead and laid to rest
Upon my final day,
The only words I wish Him to speak
Are, "In My presence stay!"

Bother if you must when I've gone the way
Of every mortal son.
Whatever you do won't matter as much
Than if He says "Well done!"

"My good and faithful servant,
My eternal rest you'll see.
Come enter my joy, mortality's done,
Be always here with Me!"

Father,

I'm having a day. I'm just not feeling it.
My faith is still strong only because You built it.
I'm having a hard time, but you've never failed me,
so, open my eyes; please help me to see.

It's me, Lord, not you. My thoughts are roaming.
The storm's in my mind, turbulent waves are foaming.
I'm at unrest. The daily news is disturbing.
People are mean and somewhat perturbing.

It's the times in which we live. I understand the tidings.
Past prophecies and now have begun their collidings.
The freight train of time barrels down the track.
Nothing can stop it nor bring it back.

I'm ready for the end. It's nearly here.
It's not the end. It's the road, I fear.
I'm under no illusions. It's about to get rough.
The signs are present with hatred and stuff.

Set me to task, put me to work.
The fields are ripe. People need You, Lord.
What can I do? How may I serve?
Busy is distracting, plus, it calms my nerves.

You know the time when in the boat You stood?
The waves heard Your voice? The winds understood?
Strengthen my resolve, quell the storm in my mind.
I want to be one in whom joy You may find.

In this moment and at this time,
as you did in the boat, please stand in my mind.
Take hold of my thoughts. Help me rein in my will.
Speak into my mind, whisper, "Peace be still!"

Your son,
David

Fish Stories

Fish stories.
War stories.
All the way to college glories.
We tell the tales,
Enthrall our friends,
While afraid to tell
Salvation's story.

We'll watch them laugh,
And make them cry,
Tell a truth or tell a lie,
When they pass by
And ask us why
Instead of tell,
we'd rather die.

So, gain some grit,
Get a fire lit,
Get up don't sit,
His Grace acquit,
When asked for a reason
Why your faith's legit,
Don't hesitate,
you should commit

It's not abstract,
Now that's a fact,
It's been your track,
How He took you back,
After sin and grief,
you'd lost the path
Of His Grace and Mercy
there was no lack.

Our efforts exhaust,
All hope was lost,
There was a cost,
Your life was tossed,
But the way was created
when the Lord aloft
Became a man,
and chose the cross.

It's God's design,
There's no more time,
It's on the line,
So get a spine,
No matter the cost,
You let His love you shine,
When you tell the tale
of God's plan divine.

Unseen, Around

I looked and saw a sea of pain
Scattered upon the ground like rain.
Broken, dirty, unwanted, unwashed,
Society's rejects, spirits squashed.

My vision clouded with tears of my own,
My heart the proverbial lake-thrown stone,
Sinking, falling, failing, stopped,
Personal sorrow, hopeless thoughts.

Walking down the unseen trail,
I wonder how I might prevail.
Feeding, clothing, minister, serve,
New laws enacted, thrown a curve.

We must find an answer within ourselves,
The ones who are left can't help themselves,
Digging deeper, money gone,
Just a man, I'm only one.

I cry out loud to any other,
"Will you help me help another?"
Water, sandwich, bag of chips,
Make the effort, I cannot quit.

Others start to answer my call,
Joining together, might we help them all?
Doubtful efforts, very rough,
More are helped, never enough.

We'll continue our efforts though weak they be,
Helping the homeless that we see.
Daily working, love unbound,
Many still there, unseen, around.

Final Day

When upon that final day,
I lay down at last to rest.
I pray the words my lips will say
Will be my very best.

I hope when death is at my door,
I'll have the chance to speak.
I'd rather be remembered more,
For praising God, though weak.

"My Lord, my God, My Savior King,
Will echo off the wall.
With my life, my praise I bring,
You are my all in all!"

With Heaven filling my spiritual sight,
As I leave this Earthly worry,
My last breath's words,
'twould be only right,
If they're the first
I finish in Glory.

Defeated

What do I do when I lose hope,
Feeling defeated and I just can't cope,
Losing my grip, trying to hold on,
Surrounded by others, yet feeling alone?

What do I do when others attack,
Out of room on the front, they stab in the back,
Gossiping and talking about nothing real,
Slaughtering my spirit with unjust speal?

What do I do when nothing goes right,
The days are all wrong, followed by darkest night,
Everything breaks, and it all loses form,
Vapor and mist, blowing winds, my norm.

So, I've had a bad week, and my dog bit me,
Even he wouldn't attend my party of pity,
My medication got dumped on the floor,
My keys were inside when I locked the door.

We love to hear about miracles and things,
Victories are easier to write songs and sing,
But life is not always easy and smooth
Every verse not sung, our souls to soothe.

There comes a time to lay aside
Weights our spirits can no longer abide,
There's a reason we don't carry the excess,
When things go wrong, and life's a mess.

Extra things when we're going through testings
Make it more difficult to see all of the blessings.
Getting rid of stuff before life goes awry
Eases the burden and clears the eye.

Whatever it is that I hold dear
When running the race, and the finish is near,
If I cling too tightly, it'll trip me up
Just let it go if I have enough.

There must be something I cannot see
That holds me back and is a burden to me.
So, help me Lord, I do not know
What holds me back and makes me slow.

What do I do when nothing is right,
Examine myself for what stops my flight?
If I can just take off and rise above
The attacks of others and of other stuff.

For now, I'm grounded, I'm here in the mud,
Arrows flung, in my heart have stuck,
But I need to run, get free, and fly
Ignore the negative and run on by.

It's hard to do if I'm weighted down.
What made me happy, now makes me frown.
So I will toss aside the things I don't need
If it's not the plant, it must be a weed.

What do I do when I feel as I do?
I'm trying so hard to always be true.
Burdens are heavy because I hold them.
Not all are wrong, necessarily a sin.

Lay them down, shrug off the pack,
Trust the Lord and never look back.
It's harder to do with things that I love,
But do it I must: set my vision above.

I cannot yet see the end of my course,
This day I must live without remorse.
There's no such thing as burden-free,
But everything is not for me.

I'm trying to get it all sorted out.
Be patient with me, I'm in a bit of a drought.
But at the end of this race, I run,
I just want to hear, "Enter in. Well done."

Why the Feet?

How precious are the feet of those,
Who carried the Word in first-century clothes.
From Egypt to Persia and Rome to Greece,
They spread the Gospel and did not cease.

Long before they breathed their last,
They were called to service no matter their past.
One at a time, He gathered them all.
Taught by actions great and small.

Working barefoot in a small boat,
A fisherman with no reputation of note.
Calloused hands, while on his knee,
Guts and scales, fresh catch from the sea.

Upscale and wealthy, tax collection his game,
Friend of sinners like him the same.
Riotous living, never too tired for fun,
Partied all night past the rising of sun.

Looking always for the promised King,
Weapons to the cause he'd happily bring.
Secrecy, intrigue, his way of life,
Prepared in a moment to take a life.

The Master called as He traveled the land,
One after another, a twelve-man band.
Called to follow and bring others in,
They had much to learn, His chosen men.

They gathered round the table long,
Ideas and thinking were very wrong.
He knew they were not meant to be
A troop of conquerors from sea to sea.

Break through their faulty thinking mind,
They would not be warriors but servant-kind.
Grabbing a bowl, He humbly knelt,
Washed their feet, and dried with felt.

Something began to change that night,
For it would not be by force or might,
That would take them to each uttermost part,
Spreading the Gospel, the Church to start.

Not a word was spoken, no one uttered sounds
As the Savior made the servant rounds.
A lesson taught and learned indeed
In one humble act, He showed their need.

Within that night, the disciples learned
Hours after their meal adjourned
To truly lead they must servant be
When on the cross their Lord they'd see.

Why "the washing of feet" would not sink in
The mind of those till freed from sin,
Three days later at the rise of sun,
Forgiveness and freedom won and done.

Fish offal, violence, party, and sin,
Were washed by the Lord on that night when
He lived an example, and set them apart
By teaching a lesson and cleansing their hearts.

How special those feet that were given a bath;
Washed and dried, set upon a path
That led them through time to reach this man,
With the message of hope, Salvation's plan.

Like those that came in a time before me
I learn by example, by what I can see.
I would not be where I am right now
Had Jesus not knelt and to others bowed.

Pride cast away, a servant I must become.
If I want to be like God's only Son.
If I want the feet that bear Good News
Like the disciples before me, I must change my views.

I've humbled my heart and renewed my mind.
Lord, set me apart to be Your servant-kind,
Spreading your message of hope and love,
May many be with me when I see You above.

Father,

I feel ill at ease.
I've lost a step.
Into my mind,
Negative thoughts have crept.

Things have gone wrong.
My feelings are hurt.
My life's in disorder.
My spirit inert.

I need movement.
I need direction.
So I cry out to You
In complete desperation.

Why do I sin
Or make mistakes
When all you've done
Is show me Grace?

At the heart of the matter
Is a matter of the heart.
The problem's never been You
From the very start.

It's always me,
Spoiled and fat,
I act like a child,
An attention-starved brat.

It's always been true.
It always has been.
My faults are my own,
My original sin.

I know the answer.
It's not hard to know.
Reliance on You
Is the way I should go.

I've been here before;
I know where to start.
Confession clears the mind,
Your forgiveness, my heart.

I cry out to You.
On this slippery slope,
Experience has taught
You're my only Hope.

So, I've confessed.
I've attempted amends.
I stand before You
Righteously cleansed.

I'm on new ground.
I've passed the past.
With You is the way,
I'll make it last.

I'll wait on Your call.
I await Your command
Having now done all,
I'll simply stand.

Just me.

The Love-Soaked Cross

Commanded to preach
to the great and the small,
Words without love
is no Gospel at all.
The Gospel is good news,
not filled with strife.
It promises abundance,
the satisfaction of life.

To speak with no longing,
leading only with sorrow,
Leaves the one who hears
with no hope for tomorrow.
The Gospel doesn't lead
to sitting in a room,
Darkened by despair
with feelings of doom.

Gripping your chair,
knuckles turned white,
Distress-filled thoughts,
and feelings of fright.
Death with a heartbeat,
life with no Spirit,
As if doing good things
will God's love merit.

The Gospel is clear
from start to ending,
His love has been there
since the very beginning.
The plan put in place
before the commencement of time,
Doesn't make sense,
it's without reason or rhyme,

If you remove love,
nothing adds up.
So put it back in,
it's more than enough.
The Word is life,
the light of all men,
Dispelling darkness,
He removes all sin.

If all you preach
is darkness and pain,
You'll leave the lost
still burdened with stain
The Gospel is hope
from finish to start,
It's the love-soaked cross
that changes a heart.

Words

It matters what we say and do,
when dealing with another.
Cold water quenches a desperate thirst,
cold words the spirit of brothers.

The words we use are clearly defined
by the actions we take in life.
What we do is the whetstone
that hones our tongues
like the useful edge of a knife.

When our actions are lacking
none can see what we say,
our words lack direction and purpose.
When we do as we say,
the expressions materialize
and the world begins to trust us.

It's a strange world today,
we can't be sure what they mean
when yelling at the top of their lungs.
Words have double meanings,
redefinition's taken place,
they speak as if in other tongues.

Now faith is the substance
of what we can't see,
it's why we know what's right.
It's far more than feelings,
beliefs or thoughts.
It's the evidence behind hope and might!

When the world attempts
to redefine faith
as less than what it is,
Our actions have spoken
much louder than words,
and our message they surely miss.

Our words unheard,
our Gospel not heeded,
it really is a shame.
Most often the fault
lies squarely on
the ones called by His name!

Repent, take action!
There's a desperate need,
our words have lost their power.
The ones who might hear,
listen, and turn
are dying by the hour!

It matters what we say and do
as we travel the road we're on,
We are responsible for what our brother does
regarding God's only Son.

My Hammer, His Hand

I did it, and I'm to blame.
Though all have sinned, like me the same.
The hand that swung hammer mightily
Belonged to no other, none other but me.

Rust and grit from stacked unuse,
Cold iron, sharpened, one purpose, abuse.
Holding nail so I could pound,
With every swing came ringing sound.

Uncoiled, cut, and knotted fast,
The rope must endure, to the end should last.
Lashing arms so flesh won't tear,
My tying - the cross-borne weight to bear.

With every selfish act not nice,
I am the soldier rolling dice.
Gambling as if nothing matters,
Doing my best to leave Grace in tatters.

In my thoughts and all I do,
I am no different, I'm just like you,
But I cannot firmly place the blame,
Except on the one who bears my name.

In spite of all my efforts best,
As I finish my work and stop to rest,
Mercy begins to fall around,
Covering my sin as Grace abounds.

My actions though very bad and rough,
His work is sufficient, more than enough.
With all my effort, I've created a flood,
It set free a stream of Grace-laden blood.

I did it. I'm sorry. It's all I can say.
What happened back then was caused by today.
The hammer, my sins of thought and deed.
Relief from depravity, my greatest need.

I'm sorry I did it, I wish I could stop.
Unable to do so, to my knees I drop.
And as I kneel upon the ground,
I just want to lay this hammer down.

There's no escape. He knew from the start
We would hold the hammer
as He holds our hearts,
So, will you join me on the ground?
You have your own; lay the hammer down.

The Mind

Infidelity begins with fantasy,
relapse with but a thought,
The journey of a thousand miles,
The direction our mind has sought.

Sin doesn't just happen,
It begins with something inside.
Out of everyone else's sight
And deep within our mind.

It is the first step of many
Down the road of doing wrong.
Imagine a deed, to think a thought,
That lingers there too long.

Just like our actions, what we think,
Has consequences for sure.
What takes place inside our minds,
Gives birth to sin's allure.

If you don't like the results
Of all the things you do,
I have a solution you ought to try:
It begins with your thoughts too.

Whatever things our Father adores,
Let your mind equally love.
Thoughts move deeds, you may be assured,
Just like a hand in glove.

If you let your mind dwell
On doing what is right
There's far less room to think the thoughts
That ends with darkness, not light.

Start each day by setting the stage
By what goes on upstairs.
Plot your course by thinking right
And always begin with prayers.

If you want to change your days
To have a better outcome,
Depend on God, control your thoughts,
Better deeds will surely be done.

But if you don't renew your mind,
With whatever is pure and more,
Your actions will only and always follow
What was there before.

It's in the Eyes

My eyes, my vision, no use since birth.
In darkness I've wandered, little humor, less mirth.
The others, they blamed my parents or me.
Sin of my forefathers, the culprit must be.

Begging became my way of life
For clothing and bread—there'd be no wife.
A miserable existence, I was bound to have.
For all my humiliation, there'd be no salve.

Along came a Man Who said night was near.
What could He know, mine was already here.
He spit in the dirt, put some mud on my eyes,
Told me to wash what He'd already applied.

The spit-laden mud I washed from my face,
I opened my eyes; the dark was erased!
An image took form in my newfound sight,
I suddenly realized the purpose of light!

Something so simple and yet so profound,
My eyes had sight as my ears had sound.
Now what I could feel had meaning to me,
What was unknown, now I could see!

The form took shape with caring eyes,
The face of a man I could never deny.
He was the first thing I saw, He changed my heart,
My life's begun, it's a brand-new start.

When cornered and questioned by the powers that be,
I replied I was blind, but now I can see.
All I knew was I had experienced Grace
From the caring eyes of a compassionate face.

As eyes are to sight, heart is to love
Hearing to ears, and purpose from above,
Without the one, there would not be the other,
Sin breaks all men; spiritual vision must suffer.

Healing is required like the man blind from birth,
For every man upon God's green Earth.
Instead of spit-mud spread upon our face,
It is blood at the foot of the cross of Grace.

Ode To Kay

My heart is heavy,
She's gone on before.
I'm outside the walls,
She's walked through the door.

A light that once shone,
Lighting paths like mine
Is now obscured
By the veil's distinct line.

The sadness I have
Is not hers to feel.
She dines with the King
Behind eternity's seal.

But I miss her words,
Wisdom and tact.
She wrote with authority,
And a faith built from fact.

Willingly she shared
From a mind and heart
Won over by Grace
To do her part.

She called me "Sonshine."
She was my "Sonbeam."
I looked for her daily.
Such was our esteem.

Like many before her
This loss causes pain.
What we will miss
Is now Heaven's gain.

The torch she carried,
Done so for the Lord,
Is too big a loss,
One we cannot afford.

I know there are others
Who will step in her place
And show the world
The light of God's Grace.

Who will it be,
And what will you do?
The Body's not whole
Without someone new.

We may have lost Kay
But we'll see her again.
We must follow her example,
And make our stand!

For now, in the present
We've been left behind,
Fighting like Kay
With a faith well-defined.

When our time is done
And we walk through the mist,
On our Lord's right hand
Will be the Kay we've missed.

The Hands of Grace

He spread His arms
in an act of Grace
To hold us all
In love's embrace.

He wept in sorrow
For the city's lost,
Sweated blood,
And paid the cost.

Do not confuse Him
With a weakling wimp,
A comedic fool,
Or a silly simp.

Just because
He shows His love
Does not mean
He's a gentle dove.

He is the lamb.
He gave His life.
He's also the Lion
That ends sin's strife.

Never forget
the nail-scarred hand
will soon draw the Sword
at Judgment's end.

So do not treat Him
With disregard;
He's earned more than that
With stripes and scars.

So as the end
Draws close and nigh,
Prepare to be called up
Into the sky.

Victory awaits
Those who decide
To stand with Him
Right by His side.

Whosoever won't
Or Whosoever will,
You may choose either
For a short while still.

Worrier or Warrior

Fool or Conqueror,
My thoughts will decide
Where I stand and on whose side.
Called Away from the Former,
And Declared the Latter.
What's in my heart
Makes a difference, it matters.
How I approach life,
what gifts I employ,
Sets my path and determines my joy.
Worrier or Warrior,
I'll not be at fault,
If He carries my burdens,
makes my life Earth's salt.

The Struggle is Real

The struggle is real.
So's the victory, indeed,
and the many miracles
that is its seed!

Dwell in the struggle,
or shelter 'neath His hand,
a life built on the Rock,
or foundations of sand.

Consequences and choices
Go hand in glove.
Life by choice,
Can be blessings from above.

Choose well this day
Whom you will serve.
Misery today,
Or eternity reserved.

From: Misery Loves Company
Wormwood Edition

What I do, don't, and say
will be mine to own on Judgment Day
And when you stand before the throne,
What is yours will be yours alone.

Don't look to blame or cast aspersions
There'll be no deflection and no diversions.
What we've done is what will be
And what will echo in eternity.

The Gospel I preach is grounded in love,
Sourced and established from God above.
One thing's for sure, though, I'd be remiss,
If I didn't provide the Heavenly list.

There are things to say and words to do
If, with some, you'll go there too.
The requirements are long and full of worry.
If you complete them all, you'll not be sorry

Love the LORD with all your heart,
With mind and body and every part.
Love your neighbor like you do yourself ...
If you have time left for yourself.

You'll be busy with much to do.
There are things to eat, memorization too.
When you wake, walk, and sleep,
Keep sin quiet, not to make a peep!

When you've done your very best,
If you want life to be very blessed,
Remember the orphans and aliens too.
For the homeless and addicts, every kindness do!

I warn you from the very start,
You must do all, not just a part,
For if you fail in one small thing,
It won't be heaven of your name sings.

Take the time and figure it out.
Salvation is not what the Law's about.
It doesn't save or even justify.
Not even I can tell that lie.

But if you think you'd prefer Grace
To rise above and see God's face,
Make sure you add something to it.
It's not hard, there's nothing to it!

Be baptized and do good deeds.
Plant, sow, and water the seeds.
Make sure you tell what you've accomplished,
How all your deeds are good and polished.

In the end, you'll fail as you must
As happens to all who end in dust.
Make sure your belief is in your action
Cause then you'll bring me great satisfaction.

Just have fun. No, have a ball!
When you fail at one, you'll fail at all.
The gates you'll bust open; I'll be there.
You can stay with me in my eternal lair.

Raca
Envoy to Churches
Lieutenant Commander
Former Light Brigade

(With tongue-in-cheek)

Writings—A Collection

The Young Couple

The young homeless couple cuddled together for warmth in the cool morning air. She was so thankful for Joe. He had been incredible, so concerned for her. She didn't know if she would have made it without him. Through no fault of their own, they were now sheltering in a barn. The economy, combined with government regulations, had left them in a bad situation in which Joe had done all he could, and that was no little thing. He was quite the handyman with wood. He had managed to stop the drafts in their newly obtained shelter.

And just in time!

She knew she would probably bear more children but didn't know how she could love another as much as she did the small bundle lying nearby, supported and sheltered by the animals' feeding trough. She was, first and foremost, a mom. She knew her child was unique. She knew all mothers felt like this, but no, this child was exceptional. God had called her blessed and given her a child, though she'd never known a man.

She laughed to herself. She was a rather practical young woman. She felt honored and humbled to be chosen, BUT it wasn't all about that. She was a mother and naturally focused on what was before her—not on all the philosophical stuff, not on all the ethereal positions. She would certainly not be arguing any great theological points of view anytime soon. She had a child to raise. And according to the whimper she just heard, he must need that diaper changed, and she was the one to do it!

****

"She's so beautiful," the somewhat older man thought. He was a bundle of emotional energy. Okay, so, yes, he had had the vision. He knew, without question, what was up. That didn't change the recriminations directed at him back home. He had attempted to be both wise and kind. At first, he had thought he couldn't accept "damaged goods," but then came the vision. She wasn't damaged; she was blessed and blessed beyond measure.

Overwhelming humility with a flood of understanding of the responsibilities before him clouded his mind, but he, too, was practical. He had a job to do. He had a role to play, but he could only do what he could do. God had chosen Mary when she was his betrothed; ergo, God had chosen him. Why? He didn't have the foggiest!

Meanwhile, he had used his knowledge to stop the cold drafts before that little bundle had arrived. At least he had correctly done that! He wondered if he would get the next thing right.

History said the time was right, and the future was a complete mystery, but he was practical. He didn't worry too much about either. He could only take life on life's terms. He was quite adept at taking things as they came. Perhaps that's why God had chosen him.

But, Mary?

She was amazing. There was no question why she had been chosen. It was hard to escape the feeling he was extra baggage, but despite his feelings, he knew better. God made no mistakes; therefore, God had chosen Joe for His reasons. Joe just hoped he'd figure out the whys and how-to's before he made a critical mistake. The burden rested heavily on his mind!

She was a young teenage mom. He was a little older but in similar straits. Both were the people God chose to parent the young Jesus. So often, we place Mary and Joseph on a pedestal as if knowing their positions meant that they intrinsically knew what to do. Scared and alone, except for Joseph, a man she was only beginning to understand, Mary, a teenager, had a natural birth in a stable. Let that sink in. Joseph, a man who conformed to Jewish tradition and law, was stumbling blindly forward because he trusted a visitation that didn't equate to the norm. After all, there was nothing ordinary about it!

Those two belong on a pedestal of sorts because of what they accomplished, but at that point where we meet them at the beginning of Luke, she is just a scared pregnant teen, and he is an older man with the weight of the world on his shoulders. Perhaps it's romantic to view Mary as this "above-the-fray," holier than the rest of us, pious, young woman who would unerringly stride into the future as the mother of the Christ!! Perhaps we view Joseph as this wise servant-man who, without question, served the needs of the "mother of God."

Yeah, probably not.

They both had individual callings, and history tells us they met the challenges laid at their feet by our Father.

But they were still just a barely wed young couple who shivered in the cold, listening to the even rhythm of the Christ child's breathing in wonder and amazement that the God of the universe would choose them. To idolize them removes responsibility for you. To place them on the proverbial pedestal at that point gives you an excuse.

Reality check. You don't have an excuse!

Make no mistake about it! The call God has placed on your life is just as significant as the one on Mary's. You're not raising Jesus, but you weren't called to.

Answer the call. You may find yourself in desperation, shivering in the cold, dark early morning hours, not knowing what the future holds, and trying to sort out your whole place in this seemingly jumbled-up mess. You'd be in good company. Do what Joseph and Mary did – take in the moment, do what needs to be done, and step into the next one. God calls faith-driven, purpose-filled, practical-minded people.

Perhaps you're one of them.

Thank God He also calls beat-up, broken down, old drug addicts on whom the world had given up. Mary and Joseph were probably the best of us. I've been the worst, and our Father called each. The importance of the calling is determined by Who calls—not the called.

Being in between, you have no excuses; fulfill your calling.

He is awaiting your call!!

The Innkeeper

"Humph!" the innkeeper griped to himself, "I'll never understand those guys!" aimlessly pointing in no particular direction.

He saw all kinds of people flow through his strategically located inn between Jerusalem and Jericho. His saving grace? He was a Jew in good standing with the uppity-ups from the Temple. He always paid his Temple taxes on time. He showed up for all the right festivals. He kept his inn segregated - half kosher, half not - so no one minded staying in his establishment.

Being a Jew, his prosperity dampened his natural disdain for anything from Samaria. The constant promise of coin sweetened his inherited distaste for their culture. The continuous traffic, bringing an endless supply of guests to the inn and diners to the restaurant, made his hatred of Samaritans bearable. After years of being in business, he tolerated the Samaritans and did so with a smile - propped up by a fat wallet!

The innkeeper had the same feelings for the Jews from Jerusalem. Their pomposity and arrogance were hard to stomach. He had been around long enough to see, despite his negativity, there were some good Samaritans. Bloodlines did not make bad people. Evil people were just evil, and the contempt he shared with other Jews didn't seem fair. Add to that, he earned the same prices for serving the Jews as he did from Samaritans, but keeping kosher food, the dining area, and sleeping rooms separated cost more. He made less for the high-born scorn of the Jews for their half-blood kindred.

But what could he do? He certainly couldn't change history, and he wasn't about to attempt altering current societal norms – not over Samaritans—but if he thought he stood a chance, he might make an effort over the money! He chuckled at the thought.

What an intriguing day it had been! The road had dragged many a wanderer in his direction! First, there had been the troop of brigands. Oh, he couldn't call them that out loud, but he knew the kind – always loud and much too free with the coin—not that he didn't appreciate the latter—but they spent like they didn't earn it. He couldn't tell whether they were Jewish or Samaritan and didn't think they cared about their targets' nationality! Whatever they were, they didn't qualify for seating on the right, and they didn't ask for it.

Besides, their coin spent like anyone else's.

Then came the self-righteous priest from the Temple's inner court. His magnanimity toward the religious ruler was evident to all present, and he sat the priest at the window on the right. He should have been an actor! It was necessary. One perceived slight, and he may as well pack it in. Even the Samaritans wouldn't darken the door of a place cursed by a priest. The innkeeper comped the meal, and he set aside a room for a few minutes' rest, though the priest would not stay long. This visitor would cost him, but it was merely the cost of doing business. To do otherwise would cost him his business.

Then came the Levite—a servant and spiritual leader of his people. He thought he recognized him from his last trip to the Temple. He was pretty sure this was the man who escorted him into the inner court. He had been nice, in a standoffish kind of way. The keeper sat him on the far right—away from the Samaritans on the left. He prided himself on knowing exactly what to do with each guest and where to seat them. The Levite was important, but not that important. He did give him a complimentary dessert.

Then, the event of the day occurred!

"Boom!" the front door slammed open. "Help me!" he heard.

Hurrying to the front, his instantaneous appraisal had him ushering to the left, for the shout had come from an obvious Samaritan. Yet another man was bundled in a Samaritan robe in the man's arms, half carried, and half dragged. As he reached the two to help, the robe fell from the bloodied face of an equally obvious Jew!

Time seemed to stop! His vision blurred and then narrowed. He stumbled as he sought to assist the uninjured man with the crime victim. How could this be?

All thoughts of which side of the room fled from the innkeeper's mind as they made their way to the front of the room nearest the fireplace. Burden lightened, the Samaritan spoke softer but with the same sense of urgency, "I will help this man tonight. I will stay by his side and bandage his wounds. However, I must be on my way tomorrow. I will pay you more than is necessary if you care for him until he can care for himself. And if needs be, I can give you more when I come back through here."

Dabbing his damp forehead with his rag, the innkeeper looked toward the swaddled package near the fireplace with the sleeping Samaritan nearby. His front room seemed a little brighter, though the fire was diminishing. His world had been rocked!! If it was anyone's responsibility to take care of his fellow Jew, it was his, and yet this low-brow, low-born Samaritan had outshone him.

The innkeeper was undone! He would never be the same. He would never look down his nose at the Samaritans again. He had seen many people that day—several who were "Righteous" in everyone's eyes. Those had been the status quo. In meeting them, nothing had changed within him. Society might dictate a divided room, but what was in his heart and mind had been forever altered by one lone Samaritan!

We often view this story looking only at the Good Samaritan's kindness and how it impacted his neighbor, the Jew. However, deeds never happen in a vacuum, and we do not only have one neighbor. Your compassion and kindness often reach further than you realize, impacting more than you see at first glance!

Who are your neighbors, and what will you do about them?

If you can't answer, I know Who will help.

He is awaiting your call!!

A Lost Gift

It had been more challenging than he had expected, but she was worth every effort!

He had nine. He but needed one more!

The young man's father picked on him but glowed with an inward pride for his son. Young love was precious but often foolish. This thing his son was doing showed great depth and maturity beyond what most young men his age displayed.

At first, he did not realize what his son was doing. At their little shop, he noticed his son examining every silver coin exchanged for goods. This had gone on for several weeks before he finally asked, "Son, what are you doing?"

The answer secretly blew him away.

"Papa, you know I'm in love with Tahor. She's perfect!"

"Only God is perfect, son, but she is impressive. You know your mother, and I approve. We're just wondering when you're going to pop the question! Have you spoken to her uncle?" the proud papa smiled.

"Not yet. You know that she has no dowry because her family is not wealthy. Her aunt and uncle raised her. At least, I'm pretty sure they cannot afford one."

"Since when do you need a girl with a dowry? We are doing quite well!" the older man grumbled.

"Papa, it's not about me! Without the dowry, she has no coins. Without the coins, she'll have no headdress showing we're married. All the other young women wear them. I will not have her duck her head in shame. I'm having the headdress made for her. I have nine perfect, shiny silver coins. I've been searching for months for the best coins. I need one more. When I speak to her uncle, I'll slip this to her as evidence of my dedication and love!"

"Foolish boy!" the proud father turned quickly so his son would not see him glow with pride. It did not bother him her family was poor. They were a good family – thrifty, hardworking, dedicated to God. She was a fine young woman. His son would be hard-pressed to do better. "Ah, young love." He thought. Come to think of it, he still had that kind of love for his wife. It was good for the parents; it would be suitable for the children.

****

She couldn't believe the blessed life she lived! She had known him since childhood. His family had done well for themselves. She knew it was not because they showed off their wealth or looked down on others but because their shop was always busy. She had been embarrassed when he came to speak with her uncle. She wasn't overly prideful; their tiny home had to be a far cry from his house on the other side of town.

Then it happened!

Adam had asked her uncle for her hand in marriage! What would her uncle say? Better yet, what would she do about a dowry? She didn't measure up. There seemed to be such a chasm between the two of them. He appeared so "together;" she felt a mess. He was a man of means; she lived a mean existence. She knew her place. She would never be his equal. She could not look the part. She certainly cared for Adam, but she almost hoped her uncle would say no.

Her uncle said, "Yes!" with a beaming smile and permitted Adam to speak with her for a moment.

She was flustered. She blushed. She'd never had trouble talking to him before, but nothing now would come out right! And, he spoke,

"Tahor, I have something for you," as he secretively slipped a package into her hands. "Please take this. I've spent months finding just the right ones for you. They're near perfect but no match for your beauty. I'd be honored if you would wear this after we're married."

With that, Adam had left her wondering what was in the small box.

****

“Noooo!” the newlywed thought. She must find it!!

She remembered that night when she had opened that box – ten perfect silver coins arranged on a beautiful silver chain. They were amazing. While she had never thought about it before, her first thought that night had been she would fit in with the rest of the women from Adam’s side of town. Upon closer inspection, she discovered she would stand out! The headdress was a fantastic gift. She had never seen one quite so beautiful!

It had been her first wedding gift. It was officially hers on the night of their marriage!

Now, there was a catastrophe! She had lost the tenth coin! It was traumatic. This was terrible. The headdress was symbolic, but it stood for all of the things she now valued as a married woman – his dedication and love, for he had provided it, and her new life, for now, she was part of a new family. There was but one thing to do!

She must find the coin!!

Somewhere along the way, as she performed her duties as the woman of the house, the coin must have fallen and rolled. She searched and searched—under the furniture, in the closets, in every corner. She didn’t want to tell Adam, but she would have no choice by the end of the day. She swept every floor. This was too important. She would not give up! Nothing else mattered throughout the day in the pursuit of the coin. She missed meals, chores were not done, and visits with friends were not made until finally, as the sun began to set, the shifting of the light in the room shimmered off the edge of the coin between the floorboards in the living room!

Relief poured through her! When Adam returned from his busy day, the lights were brightly lit, fresh flowers adorned the tables, and their friends had gathered for a celebration meal.

The young bride had recovered the lost coin!!

****

And the Kingdom of Heaven is like the lost coin. We must pursue it with everything we have!!

I find it interesting. The Fruit of the Spirit is love, joy, peace, patience, kindness, goodness, faithfulness, gentleness, and self-control—nine parts that lead to a tenth—the Satisfaction of Life or the Abundant Life.

We are the bride. He is the Groom. We wear what He provides. The Fruit is a gift given upon our marriage to Him – our Salvation.

If you are not yet connected, cease and desist everything in your life.

He is worth it all.

If you've lost a coin, stop what you're doing and pursue it with all that you are – with all you have.

Nothing else matters.

He is awaiting your call!!

The Boy

“Hey, lover boy! It’s about time you got here.” And the men laughed together.

The young man hated it when his brothers called him “lover boy.” It went with the territory. He was their little brother. What else would they do but pick on him?! The friendly harassment was usually well received. They were a tight-knit family. Now, they had been separated by war; even so, brotherly comradery could not be erased by the daily trials on the frontlines.

“Why couldn’t Dad have named me anything else?!” the young man grumbled under his breath as he handed the supplies over to the older siblings. His name just begged to be misused! As he turned to leave, the raucous sounds of the military encampment suddenly ceased, and he heard a cry.

“Hey, everybody. He’s at it again!” the young man heard the nervous cry wobble through the air like a warped arrow.

The encampment emptied; soldiers rushed to the high ground above the battlefield. Not one who enjoyed being left behind because it had happened all too often, the young man followed the troops. Peering around a boulder, his eyes found their target, and his heart skipped a beat. He had never before seen such a man! Hair slicked back and oiled with a ponytail bound by multiple leather rings, hairy arms with a spear held in one hand and a sword in the other, a shield the size of a chariot wheel strapped on his back, a monstrous man stood on the field with a look of pure hatred on his face that threatened to curdle the young man’s blood.

The young man felt a hand on his shoulder, and a voice whispered in his ear, “You need to go back to your sheep, little brother. Things might go bad quickly, and you shouldn’t be here if they do.”

Shrugging the hand from his shoulder, the shepherd looked back at his brother and past him. The giant below had been shocking, but what he saw around him galvanized his fear into anger! His brothers and all of the troops cowered behind stones! So much for the machismo, he'd always heard from the older men. He understood the fear; he was afraid himself, but there was no way he would fear a heathen Philistine!

The young shepherd's assessment was interrupted by a deep, growling voice echoing off the valley walls, "You're nothing but dogs, and the God you serve is one too!"

Well, that just wouldn't do! The shepherd boy who would be king, David, whose name means beloved, had had enough. A life on the range had taught him a few things about himself, but more importantly, it had taught him much about God—the God He served.

After trying on armor that didn't fit and listening to advice from people hiding behind the rocks, David made the proclamation, "I have faced down a bear and a lion, and my God has protected me from harm. The man may be large, but my God is bigger!" (or something like that). Finally, David did his homework, learned about his enemy, and went to the stream flowing across the valley. He chose five stones, put them in his bag, and made his way to stand before Goliath. After the giant's challenge, David told him precisely what would happen and charged toward his enemy.

Of course, we know the story. It's probably one of the best-known, most loved stories in the Old Testament. David felled Goliath with a single shot, as he had known he would.

But wait! David had secured five stones from the creek bed. What do you mean, "as he had known he would?!"

It's a little-known Biblical fact. Ask most people, and they'll say he was being prepared. Yep, they are right on that fact, wrong on the substance.

Speaking of substance, "Now faith is the substance of things hoped for and the evidence of things not seen." David had faith. He proclaimed it on the field that day. "This day, God, the God who you defiled, will conquer you." The shepherd who would become the most beloved ruler in Jewish history didn't plan on missing. He didn't reach in his bag and pull out two stones as he charged a man twice his size in case he erred because the battle was the Lord's. He knew God. He had the substance of having experienced God's protection. He had the evidence of slain predators that had gone after his flock. Because he had seen it before, he knew where his stone would go, and his faith was not in his ability. It was in the Lord God!

David entered the duel with one stone for Goliath and four for Goliath's brothers! Some might call that overconfidence. Can one be overconfident of our Heavenly Father? I think not. I know not, and so did David. To him, Goliath was already defeated, and he was looking forward to further victories.

Now, that's faith!

Then the most amazing thing happened! Isn't that how it goes? When one displays true faith – a faith built upon substance and evidence – it sparks something in others. It inspires people. Perhaps it shames them, but for whatever reason, people get motivated. The spark of David's faith ignited a flaming conflagration of valor. What had been physical fear became a spiritual juggernaut that propelled God's people forward to victory. The Jewish troops leaped from behind the rocks and pursued with great haste the objects of their fear, and their enemies fled before them. Ultimately, although not all in that day, the other four giants of Gath were slain – and none of them by David. They were all killed by men previously hidden in fear behind rocks off the battlefield! They had not even been engaged, yet they became giant slayers!

What kind of battles are you facing? Are you a David ready to put your faith on the line? Are you cowering behind rocks, not even engaged in the fight? If you're a David, your actions will have consequences. They may spark a blaze that sets the world on fire for our Lord. If you've been hiding, afraid of the contest, it's okay. The battle is the Lord's; you can still be a giant slayer.

It's time to exercise some faith in your life. When has God ever failed? Put that sure knowledge into action and become the slayer of giants!

He is awaiting your call!!

The Island in the River

Life is a river with no bank on either side that flows to a waterfall at the center that ends in eternity. If you stay on the river, you will plunge at the end. There is no escape from the river. The river is placid in places, and depending on how you navigate or where you start, it may be easier for some, but the drop is unavoidable for all.

Imagine, if you will, the rapids as you approach the waterfall. In the middle of the stream is a rock island. It may even appear foreboding to some, but it is all the river offers except the depths beyond. After all, it is a rock, and it has to be stronger than the water to survive the torrents of the rapids. If you approach with respect for the rocks, you may land. If you disregard it, your boat will be battered and broken to pieces before being pushed over the edge into the abyss. You can ignore the island altogether, preferring to go around, but as I said, the waterfall is unavoidable.

As you near the island, someone on the shore may offer their hand. You may pause and listen to what they say. "There's life here! Once you land and go beyond what you can see, abundance is in the middle of the island. Taste the fruit we've grown. It is good," as they offer you a bite. "If you continue, there's a nasty waterfall you cannot escape. If you trust the Rock, you'll have life and life more abundantly! If you don't, there's no other hope."

"Why are you down here?" you might ask.

"What we have is amazing. I'm grateful and want to share it with all who pass by because going where you are headed will not end well."

"But isn't it dangerous for you to be here? This is kind of crazy for you, and I see your food, but I can't see how you grow anything on this rock!"

"Ah, there are others here with me. They produce what I give so that I can offer it to you. Yes, it's dangerous, but what I offer is worth sharing. I've stood on the top of the island. I've seen what's ahead. There's no other hope for you."

Recognizing the truth in his words, you decide to hang around, but despite the evidence that there's more to the island than you can readily see, you don't land. You work your boat around to the back side of the island out of the swift current. You interact with the people of the island. They help you with boat repairs. They encourage and feed you from their abundance, but still, you stay on the river.

One day, a storm blows in. The river rises and becomes rough. Those on the island endure the same weather, but the waters threaten to push you towards the waterfall just out of sight. The islanders struggle to keep you lashed to the island. Some even get hurt in the process.

"See!" you say, "The storm's just as bad on you. Look at you. You're as battered as I am."

"My friend, the river impacts all of us. It's the river, but even during the storm, we can go to the island's center. You've never been here. You don't understand. In fact, most of our hurts come from being here to help you, but we gladly accept that risk because we know how good island living is. If you trust the island, you'll be better for it, and maybe some of us can spend more time in the center. The river is full of travelers, so once we get you off that boat, you'll find safety, and we can help another. After you've visited the center, I'm sure you'll feel the same way we do and spend some time on the rocks rescuing others. But, if you don't step on the land, you'll never understand what's over the hillside. It's so much better."

When the next storm comes, as the rope breaks securing your boat, you leap for the hands of the islanders, and you step for the first time on the Rock.

"What? The ground doesn't move beneath my feet. I can hardly walk."

"I understand. Remember, I, too, came from the river. You'll discover it's a lot easier with firm ground beneath you. It may seem difficult initially because you're used to fighting to stay balanced. On the island, you only have to trust the Rock. It doesn't move, and it's much easier to walk when you figure that out! Come, let's go to the center!"

As you crest the hilltop bordering the rocky shore, you begin to glimpse the life you can lead. Rocky shores are replaced with farmland and houses made to shelter. The storm is still blowing, but balance is more manageable, sustenance plentiful, and you begin to understand why the islanders are so joyful.

On the way, you may have passed former travelers who were happy to be off the river but never ventured inland and built their homes on the rocky shore. Still battered by the river, they were happy just being on solid ground, but they missed the full bounty of island living by never venturing inland.

Others still moved inward but refused to eat the crops grown in the rich farmland, preferring fare from the river. They were not as happy and healthy, but like the shore people, they were islanders.

"I'm so glad you joined us. Go as far in as you'd like. My home is at the center. There's plenty of room for you there, too. I go home often, but experiencing all the island has to offer, I often go to the shore for travelers like you, for I have too much; I can't help but give it away. If I didn't share from the farm where I grow my crops, I'm afraid it would spoil in my cupboards. The island provides all I need and much, much more. You'll see if you travel to the center, but that is a journey you must take. Just like I had to convince you to get out of your boat, you have to decide how you want to live – poor like the shore dwellers, unhappy and unhealthy like the others you've passed, or with more than you can contain for yourself. The island has saved you. Your abundance is up to you. It's all here within your reach.

"We're all still travelers, and eternity still waits, but it's not in the abyss beyond the falls. From the island is a bridge to the far side of the waterfall. It's the final benefit of dwelling on the Rock, but the island's abundance is here for you now. You need never fear the river or the waterfall again."

He is awaiting your call!!

On Defining the Impossibly Contained

I got angry today. I'm kind of out of sorts, anyway. It didn't take much to shove me over the edge.

So, someone who claims to defend the Gospel posted an attack against a praise and worship song. He didn't like calling God's love "reckless."

Now, I'm a word guy. I love maintaining definitions for clarity's sake. It seems all the fad to redefine words and history in the "woke age" to suit someone's purposes. I despise that!

I'm also a poet, and I love to draw images with prose, eliciting certain emotions through word choice, so I'll stretch the meaning or lean heavily into a particular nuance.

I come by that, honestly, by the way. My favorite textbook and awesome Tutor do the same thing!

Sticking only to strict Pharisaical definitions will get you in quite a bit of trouble.

Does God possess any foolishness or weaknesses? Because the foolishness of God is wiser than men, and the weakness of God is stronger than men. I Corinthians 1:25.

Does the Good Shepherd pursue each lost sheep, or is He closer than our breath inside of us, or do we search for God while He may be found, or is He knocking at the door? Matthew 18, John 10, Psalm 34:38, Isaiah 55:6-7, Revelation 3:20.

I can go on, but you get my point.

As God seeks to mature us, He will use every nuance and reach deeper into our finite language to describe Himself in ways we can understand, for how can the limited know the Unlimited if He does not meet us where we are by stretching the boundaries of our comprehension? After all, He chose a name that describes Himself perfectly, for I AM has no limitations. It was His introduction to us, and everything since has been His work to draw us to Him. History is His story of the loving pursuit by the Creator of His creation. That pursuit came at unfathomable costs we cannot comprehend. He became a man, chose to live with limitations, faced every temptation, endured betrayal, suffered death, and overcame death and Hell by His blood.

That sure appears reckless to me. Yes, He knew the outcome beforehand, but He chose that path for us, our redemption, and our growth towards Him. He could have done it any way He wanted, but He declared by choice, "Greater Love hath no man but to lay down his life for his friends." He set the bar high and met every challenge. He has no limits, no boundaries. What more could we understand than laying His life on the line for us? Isn't that the most? And He did it.

We're supposed to be like Him.

We know the end. It's not hidden from us at all. Yet, many of us would call it reckless to go into the ghetto, the homeless encampment deep in the woods, or the war zone overseas to reach the lost. Shoot, I do it! You should see some of the places I've been almost scarred witless with knees literally knocking, muttering prayers under my breath, and yes, I call myself reckless sometimes.

He left the perfection of Heaven into this mess we've made of His creation. He wept. He prayed so fervently He sweated drops of blood, "Father, if this cup can pass from Me…". He did so with reckless abandon for the safety of Himself. He had yet to endure the lashes of the whip, the abandonment by His followers, and the pounding of the nails into hands and feet. Knowing what was coming, He threw all caution for self-preservation aside and laid it all out for us. Before He pronounced, "It is finished!" could He have wondered how much more He would have to endure?

Sounds like reckless love to me.

If we were viewing it from eternity's side, it wasn't reckless, but Christ chose to view things from our side. I think it's okay to express the infinite as best we can in our finite language – even stretching it at times to elicit an emotional response and deepen our understanding. We cannot understand God if we do not see through the eyes of Christ. Jesus is the culmination of the introduction He made at the burning bush.

All of this to ask, when was the last time you sought the lost at every cost? We know the end, but in my experience, it doesn't lessen the fear or the pain. It requires that confident yet reckless abandon Jesus possessed as He placed the ear back on the soldier, healing him, and was marched back into the city.

Those muttered prayers do help, by the way.

He is awaiting your call!!

I Need A Lyre

What a disaster!

"Politics!" the old leader thought so loudly that the thoughts almost pierced the ethereal silence beside the river. When would his son ever learn?

Skipping a rock over the silent waters into a shoal, the king reminisced. His life had been far more like the rapids upstream than the shoal. It certainly wasn't like the quiet waters around the deep but rocky-bottomed shoal at the end of the skipping rock's journey.

How quickly his king had forgotten his service in that hot, dusty valley so long ago! After his king's death, he remembered ascending to the throne. He had won victory after victory. When he was long gone, the next king would have few enemies about which to worry. He had handled the nation's business!

All, apparently, had forgotten - including his own.

He had failed within the walls of his own home. His children constantly bickered. One of his sons had raped one of his daughters. Another son killed the rapist. They were out of control! And, now? Now, he'd been run out of his palace and capital by one of his children!!

Could things have gotten any worse-so much for living up to his name's meaning? He felt far from beloved. David had seen disappointment too many times. He knew our Father's answer was on the far side of the trouble. He just had to get there, and the journey would not be easy. It would require submission. It would demand repentance. It would need a Recognition of his own weakness. And his praise to God, as always, would be a necessary component.

As the Jordan flowed seamlessly past his perch toward the shoals, David reached for his battered, well-loved lyre and began to sing:

"Oh, LORD, my enemies are too many to count. They have joined forces against me!

Right in my face, they tell me, "God's given up on you. You're not worth saving."

But, You, LORD, Who has no beginning nor ending, wrap Yourself around me like an impenetrable shield. You give me the glory I do not deserve, and when, embarrassed at my losses and, I can't even look up, You gently pull my face to look up to You. I lift my voice to You, my LORD, and You answer me!"

It was not a song of blind hope. They were words of praise built on David's life experience. He knew God, and he knew God didn't bring him that far to leave him. Sound knowledge of remembrances gone by drove his mind and will - particularly when things were down. He knew he had forgotten God too many times to count. Likewise, he knew God had never forgotten him.

Without knowing how the story would end, without knowledge of what would happen to Absalom, sitting beside the river, in great sadness, dusty and dirty from fleeing Jerusalem in fear, David resorted to praise.

I'm looking for my lyre, harp, or something.

He is awaiting our praise!!

A Long Time Ago in a Faraway Land ...

"Dad, how're you going to build here? There are too many trees, and it stinks! Why would you choose this place?"

"Son, there are lots of reasons. The biggest is, this area is big enough and flat enough for what we need. Now, grab the other side of the saw. We've got to get this area cleared."

"That's my point! Before we can build, we have to clear it first! There are too many trees!"

"That's my point, son. We're going to use these trees in the construction."

"Oh! I understand. Once we cut them down, we won't have to move them very far to use them. It just looks like an awful lot of trees."

"We need an 'awful lot' of wood, to use your phrase," the elder man said with a smile as the first tree fell.

"But, Dad, it stinks! Couldn't we have built somewhere other than next to a tar pit?"

"The tar is another necessary component of what we're doing. Can you imagine toting that smelly stuff for a long way, and by the time you got to where you're going, it'd probably have cooled down? We'd have to heat it back up, and you'd have to deal with the smell anyway."

"I'd ask about the creek running right through the middle of the job site, but you'd probably tell me we need mud."

"Smart boy! We do need mud, freshwater, somewhere to tan hides, cure and curve wood for barrels, and water the livestock. Yes, we need the stream. Everything you see as an obstacle is actually a benefit!

Accomplishing what the LORD has commanded requires these obstacles/benefits. When doing anything, we first have to use what God gives us, and the greatest, past the willingness to obey, is our brains. And Shem?"

"Yeah, Dad?"

"You can start debarking that first tree."

The young man glanced over at his two younger brothers playing in the stream, looked a third of a mile towards the end of the area his father had marked out, grabbed the double-handle draw-shave, and began removing the bark from the first tree.

There would be hundreds more before the area was clear and thousands more before Noah finished the Ark. His three sons would be grown and married, and he would be gray with age.

But it all began with the first tree and, perhaps, 1001 questions by his oldest son!

Ramblings of a Man Surprised and Forever Altered by Joy

Most people anxiously await, as if whatever is coming should be a thing to fear with great trepidation. I have learned that I have nothing to fear from the hand of our Lord, and joy is found in the destination and the journey! So, I have discovered a life of joy is one of expectant anticipation.

Anxieties and fears are perilous trip-traps along the way into which we stumble not by the action of the feet. Still, instead, we tumble and fall, losing our balance, when we look away from the Hope He has secured in our hearts - a confident hope bound to the realities of the substance and evidence that are the building blocks of our faith! It is an action of the eye as we lose sight of fact and drift into the malaise of doubt when we know better through previous experience. It is an effort of our minds we actively choose when we gaze with desire into the pitfalls of anxiety. It is spiritual movement as we slip down the proverbial greased skids, plunging headlong into the selfish desire and hedonistic, wanton pleasure of the stasis of a settled life devoid of incorporeal, forward-moving purpose anchored beyond our existence.

Now, life happens, and it happens to everyone, great and humble. How it hits us is determined by Who is with us - both physically and spiritually.

I've seen so much from His Graceful hand. It has blown me away; so much of my anxiety has evaporated into a confident, almost prescient, and hopeful expectancy. Life, overall, has become something of profound joy, birthing each second as if there'd never been a moment quite like that one before.

I think C.S. Lewis entitled his book well, Surprised by Joy, where he penned beautiful sentiments like:

"All Joy reminds. It is never a possession, always a desire for something longer ago or further away or still 'about to be.'" (Notice the expectancy part)?

And,

"But who can duly adore that Love which will open the high gates to a prodigal who is brought in kicking, struggling, resentful, and darting his eyes in every direction for a chance of escape? The words "compelle intrare," compel them to come in, have been so abused by wicked men that we shudder at them, but, properly understood, they plumb the depth of the Divine mercy. The hardness of God is kinder than the softness of men, and His compulsion is our liberation-" something to be desired but not yet attained.

When we've found it, not even the woes of COVID resurgence or terrorist attacks can attack a foundation anchored in the Rock, for He is Joy itself, and a great building rises from its foundation. But I have to say, it is trying. Ugh.

There's a reason why the night is darkest before dawn. We appreciate the morning so much more, and our Father loves to show off His love in the breaking of the day! I've learned that no matter the darkness of night, the dawn is always worth waiting to see joyfully bursting over the horizon.

Pregnant with expectation and with bated breath, I have determined to look forever forward to the next amazing thing. It's coming. There is no doubt. The only real question is, "How much will He blow me away this time!"

No matter where He takes you, bask in each pinpointed intersection of time and space and wring the joy out of it as a deserted man squeezes a water-sodden bandana for that last drop. Crush the bandana of the moment as much as you like, and you'll reveal to yourself and all around you that there's no end to the refreshment. You'll only move into the next second, not because you found the boundaries of joy, but with expectancy because the last was never-ending, and the next has to be more.

He is awaiting your call!!

Dear Friend,

I hope you enjoyed the poems and writings! One that has particularly meant a great deal to me is "Unseen, Around." I penned it as I struggled with the homeless plight in Austin, TX, a couple of years ago. It is an issue that remains near and dear to my heart.

I am currently on a five-year mission trip across the United States, working with churches to reach the Forgotten Ones of society. I would like to invite you to join me—not literally in the RV. It wouldn't take much to fill this thing up! No, I would love to visit your community with a message of hope for both your community at large and the disenfranchised who dwell around you. We have the answer. We can end homelessness and addiction, and bring healing to the disconnected, but it will be one relationship with Christ at the time!

Join me by donating to the Forgotten Ones Crusade—the link is on my website at **thebakerandthebread.com.**

You can purchase books and bible studies for prisoners, homeless survival kits, care packages for nursing homes, and help fund our outreach.

Most importantly, you can join me in the streets and involve your local church. You may reach me at

David.Riordan@thebakerandthebread.com

Or on **The New Baker and the Bread**

on Facebook. I look forward to seeing you there!

In Christ Alone,
David

PS: Always make your Amazon purchases through the link on my website to support the Crusade! A portion of every purchase is set aside for the Forgotten Ones Crusade as long as you enter Amazon through my link.

Also By The Author on Amazon

Beginnings

https://amzn.to/3FuJbax

David Riordan is a missionary to the Forgotten Ones of society: the homeless, disenfranchised, and disconnected, but he has not always been. God met him where he was in the middle of his mess, in the middle of the storm of his life, and rescued him. In his first book, The Baker: Prelude to a New Kind of Life, he details those most consequential days, but what gave rise to the necessity of God's move in his life? What was the Prequel to the Prelude to the life he now lives

From the highs and lows of life to the literal highs and lows of a life plagued by addiction, Riordan recounts a life spiraling out of control to the point his life hung in the balance. Intelligent, with his wits eventually stretched to their limits, he entered into a deal to save one for whom he cared greatly. From accidents to attempts on his life and drug deals to gun running, he operated on the edge of a life few ever visit, and most would not have survived. Had God not intervened, neither would have he.

This is the story of his Beginnings.

The Seed, The Gardener, The Servant

https://amzn.to/3QpAtRf

An endearing illustrated story of the life and times of a very special dogwood tree.
Follow the tale of unexpected trials
and the journey to expectant anticipation
under the care of the Gardener,
as the seed, come tree, discovers purpose
and fulfillment as part
of a greater plan.

The Baker: Prelude to a New Kind of Life

https://amzn.to/406p0Ju

"I was living on the edge—
not within the margins of the past year—
but on the precipice of now."

The Baker: Prelude to a New kind of Life is an incredible story of one man's journey from darkness to light. A recovering drug addict who volunteered to go undercover to help his nephew receive a lesser sentence, David soon found himself running for his life. After having been beaten nearly to death in a drug deal gone wrong, with his life in jeopardy, he set off on foot.

This is the story of a grueling four-day journey that took David from Griffin, Georgia to Boston, Massachusetts. Through storm and cold, privation, and threats, God's loving hand guided him to healing and redemption by the power of His love. Miracle after miracle experienced by the most unlikely of characters, David simply chose to put God first, leaving all else behind.

Open the pages and step into the captivating tale of one man's journey of deliverance through God's redeeming mercy. The Baker-Prelude will touch every reader's heart and soul, demonstrating that our God is real and very much alive!

Excerpt from Beginnings: The Baker's Story, My Saga

Writing a memoir is, I'm sure, a lot different from, say, a novel. In fiction, one must think about the plot, devise the twists and turns of the story, and invent people. I'm sure that is a painstaking process. I have yet to find out. I've never done it. So, I don't know what a novelist or writer goes through when writing.

I am not a novelist, and other writers worldwide are likely glad to hear me say I'm not like them.

This is not a novel. I wrote most of this story in May, June, and July 2018. I froze when I got to the final line of the last chapter about the following Tuesday. It is not writer's block. I haven't suddenly lost the ability to write; I have posted over 400 blogs amounting to 400k+ words since then.

It is fear.

At this point, I had already begun to push the envelope. I was living on the edge, but my fear was not of some of the people I encountered. They were dangerous, and some harmed me, but time has elapsed, and my faith and walk with Christ have removed most of the fear. Time may heal, but I serve the greatest Healer, and He is also my Protector. So, no, my fear is not of evil people. They hold no power over me anymore.

My fear is not for people I knew either. A good number of them have found sobriety and now follow my blog. Their lives are no longer my responsibility. If they are still in "the life," I can only pray for them. If there are those in law enforcement who, either by design or in ignorance, seek to harm me, it is also in my Father's hands. I have learned to rely entirely on Him.

No, my fear is in the writing, for unlike a novel, I do not have to contrive a plot. Unlike a fictional account, I do not have to make up characters for my story. Unlike a novel, I do not write for pleasure.

I write to tell the story but to tell it, I must relive it.

The redemption that comes later is easy. While some might bring personal anguish and regret, my ancient memories from earlier life have receded from prominence in my mind. Even writing about my life on the edge was simple enough.

What happens next in my story remains a wound—oozing with potential infection. Over two years later, I had to change the spiritual bandages and apply more ointment of prayer. It broke something deep inside me, requiring a long time to heal. This part of my story changed everything, for after the events of the coming Tuesday, I made yet another choice. I was no longer living on the edge. I leaped into the chasm. I dove into Alice's rabbit hole, as it were. I had only one choice, one option ahead, and it was an all-or-nothing proposition.

There was no way I would come out unscathed, and a strong likelihood I might not make it out, but while I might have had other choices, they were all untenable.

This is not a novel. This is not fiction. I am not crafting a story. It was all too real, and as I write, I must dredge up memories, and in the process, I must relive them.

So, it is the writing I fear. The experiences were bad enough, and I lived in terror at points. My mistakes, and thus, my regret, must be felt all over again. But the hardest part? The great sadness reconstituting from memory seeks to pull my soul to the depths as if an anchor were tied about my waist while attempting to swim the world's oceans. So, I find myself, in the writing, stumbling about in the darkness all over again, devoid of hope, fearing my actions, in the end, would be pointless.

****

The day arrived. As I approached the day, I had no great sense of anxiousness. I had done all the necessary work. I had the youngest's school situation lined up. I had done everything. No one should be able to say anything too damaging. I had my probation officer's backing. Besides, this hearing was supposed to be a formality. My older daughter, who had guardianship, had vocalized support for Grace returning home with me. Everything was good.

Or so I thought.

The first sign I should have noticed was my ex-wife's attitude. There was nothing unusual about her attitude. She wanted others to view her favorably, but she commonly wanted to do something other than what she needed to achieve that. She haphazardly paid child support and didn't make time for the kids, but she didn't want to see me win—as she viewed it—ignoring that it wasn't about me winning; it was about what was best for our youngest.

We took the conversation outside.

"Look, it's relatively straightforward. This is a formality. If you try to insert garbage into this proceeding, I'll tell the judge the truth. You're behind thousands of dollars in child support to me and the same to Lydia, and you never see the kids, though nobody is stopping you. I have even facilitated you seeing them despite you many times. That's the unadulterated truth. Like it or not!"

"Stop trying to intimidate me. You're intimidating me!"

"Intimidating you with the truth? Perhaps you should examine your life."

Her ex-counselor husband yelled at me from the door, "You better stop intimidating her!" It must have been a prearranged script since he could not hear our conversation.

I went back inside, shaking my head, but I should have realized that with a prearranged script, something was afoot.

The crowd in the court waiting room seemed to grow larger. People who had no direct reason for being there were beginning to arrive. It should have made me nervous. Not perceiving made what was to come so much more surprising.

Sucker-punch: "A true sucker punch is quite a bit more complex than a simple unannounced attack. It primarily involves a closed fist contacting the soft underbelly of a person, … (which) leaves the victim open to various other attacks. (UrbanDictionary.com)

I had assumed others had been honest with me; an assumption, combined with exhaustion from my current extracurricular efforts, left me with my guard down. Believing this to be a formality, I had already lost before the day began.

The clerk called my case, and everyone filed into the courtroom. The sucker punch landed almost immediately.

"I'm Judge ****. Does anyone have any questions before we get started?"

I don't remember what my question was going to be, oh, but I do remember the judge's response to my raised hand.

"You, sir, don't open your mouth in my courtroom!"

I was not the only one who had filled out paperwork before the day. It was clear who was responsible for directing the blow—my daughter, L, who then used the bulk of the time tearing into me and whose attacks went unabated by the judge. Yes, the person who had proclaimed her support to my face had delivered the blow.

I do not know who she had managed to convince to write the court against me, but I have figured some of it out. Whoever wrote, it doesn't matter. The damage was done. I had already been shut down in my own hearing, and this was the juvenile court where the judge is the potentate. This king exercises his authority without due process and on his whim. I did not get to face my accusers or even find out the accusations. I had no opportunity to offer a defense. I was proverbially hauled out and lynched.

The blow had been deadly to me. In no uncertain terms, the judge told me I would never have my children again.

While I would never wish evil on anyone, had I not already run off and started doing what God had laid out for me to do on my own, had I been standing firmly in my faith, I would have seen God's hand at work beginning immediately after that farce of a hearing. Still, I had left God's path and wasn't standing on a firm foundation.

Instead, I was left demolished, crushed, defeated, and looking for solutions alone; I took the plunge. Instead, I missed everything God did. What happened in court was ugly, and as a friend once said, "God doesn't like ugly!"

For those who did the wrong thing, their lives spun into disaster and chaos. I'm under no illusions I'm different from God's other children. When He adopts us into his family, He takes care of us—in blessings, discipline, and revenge (vengeance is never our call to make). I have been on the receiving end of it all.

Had I been the least bit plugged into my Heavenly Father, I would have seen His swift action as the house of cards in my opponents' lives began to crumble. But, instead, I missed it all. I was too wrapped up in myself, and I missed learning something I have since learned, for in spinning off even further on my own, the chaos that would ensue in my life would leave me with no choices, as you will soon discover.

The first one was arrested at the courtroom door for an obscure warrant from years before and spent months in jail. Jobs were lost. Psychological problems went into full bloom, and financial ruin threatened a few. And I do not make light of it. Nevertheless, it would have been better if we had done the right thing.

Regrettably, not one did—including me.

Devastated, I crossed the parking lot to my vehicle and got in. I sat as my mind roiled in dismay and confusion. The work I had been doing had played a part in my destruction. Nobody knew. Nobody could know. However, if I had any hope of ever countering what went on in court, it would be me proving I had contributed something positive to my community, thereby gaining the endorsement of law enforcement.

It was no longer simply about my young friend, Vick. That was my primary goal, but I would have to cast my net wider. The sheriff's department had already offered to pay me, and the DEA proposed a similar arrangement, but I had turned it all down.

They continued to say many things. I would continue to turn money down, but I clung to one promise. They committed to expunge my record because I had gone above and beyond, and in the process, I hoped to gain favor with the juvenile court.

It may seem convoluted to you, but I saw no other options. So, I decided in the middle of the parking lot of the Juvenile Court on Solomon Street. I would do whatever it took. I would be willing to do anything.

I would have to be viewed as a hero to the good guys, but there was only one way I could obtain the information I needed. I would have to get my hands dirtier and go deeper than what I had been going, and I got the blessings of Victor C.

"If you're in the county, it'll be no problem. I'll make sure charges are never filed if you're picked up, and if you're outside the county, you might have to sit in jail for a few hours until I can pick you up. We have a good relationship with all the surrounding counties, so you'll be alright."

I'm not stupid. I didn't trust law enforcement any more than the drug dealers. I figured Victor C. was good for his word, but I knew he had limits despite what he said. Again, though, I would have nothing to worry about as long as I produced.

I drove home angry and frustrated. Then I called my control officer, Victor C., and Vick, with the same message to both.

"I'm outta court. Let's do this thing!"

The deeper I went, the darker it became.

Made in the USA
Monee, IL
08 November 2023

45961508R00060